P9-DTI-784

The Statue
of Liberty

CORNERSTONES
OF FREEDOM™

SECOND SERIES

Elaine Landau

Children's Press®
A Division of Scholastic Inc.
New York • Toronto • London • Auckland • Sydney
Mexico City • New Delhi • Hong Kong
Danbury, Connecticut

Photographs ©2004: AP/Wide World Photos/George Widman: 41; Corbis Images: 5, 24 (Bettmann), cover bottom (Joseph Sohm/ChromoSohm Inc.), 22 (Cathy Crawford), 38, 39, 44 (Jim Erickson), 3, 45 (Museum of the City of New York), 33 (Alan Schein), 14; Folio, Inc.: 4, 44 (Jeff Greenberg), 7 left (Lelia Hendren); Free Library of Philadelphia: 20; Getty Images/Andrew Ward/Life File: 19 left; Hulton|Archive/Getty Images: 28; Library of Congress: 12, 13, 17, 23, 34, 35; Museum of the City of New York: 15; NYC & Company: 40, 45; New York Public Library Picture Collection: 31; North Wind Picture Archives: 25, 32, 45; Rigoberto Quinteros: 36; Statue of Liberty National Monument/National Park Service: cover top, 6, 7 right, 9, 10, 11, 18, 19 right, 21, 27, 29, 30, 37, 44, 45; Yale University Art Gallery/Joseph Szaszfai: 8.

Library of Congress Cataloging-in-Publication Data
Landau, Elaine.
  The Statue of Liberty / Elaine Landau.
    p. cm. — (Cornerstones of freedom. Second series)
Summary: Briefly tells the story of the Statue of Liberty, from when the idea was born, how the statue was built, and information about the creator.
  Includes bibliographical references (p.) and index.
    ISBN 0-516-24233-4
    1. Statue of Liberty (New York, N.Y.)—Juvenile literature. 2. New York (N.Y.)—Buildings, structures, etc.—Juvenile literature. [1. Statue of Liberty (New York, N.Y.) 2. New York (N.Y.)—Buildings, structures, etc.] I. Title. II. Series.
F128.64.L6L36 2003
974.7'1—dc21

                                                    2003009096

CHILDREN'S PRESS, and CORNERSTONES OF FREEDOM™, and associated logos are trademarks and or registered trademarks of Scholastic Library Publishing. SCHOLASTIC and associated logos are trademarks and or registered trademarks of Scholastic Inc.

1 2 3 4 5 6 7 8 9 10 R 13 12 11 10 09 08 07 06 05 04

OCTOBER 28, 1886, WAS A damp, chilly day in New York City. A cold wind swept over New York Harbor, hinting that a freezing winter was on its way. Yet that didn't stop a large crowd from gathering for an event that had been years in the making. In addition, more than three hundred boats had arrived in the harbor for the occasion. Their crisp white sails formed a patchwork against the choppy gray water.

What began as a gift of international friendship would soon become an enduring symbol of freedom and democracy.

On land, New York City's mayor and the state governor began to take their seats. United States President Grover Cleveland also arrived to give the speech of the day. Nevertheless, none of these officials was the star of the event. The excitement was not about a person, but a statue. Everyone was there for the **dedication** of a huge **monument** named

"Liberty Enlightening the World," more commonly known today as the Statue of Liberty.

The 151-foot (46-meter) copper structure was indeed a magnificent sight. Taking the form of the Roman goddess of Liberty—Libertas—the statue holds a torch lighting the way to liberty. The broken shackles at the statue's feet stand for freedom from **tyranny**. The law tablet in her left hand represents the Declaration of Independence and the American ideal that "all men are created equal."

Surrounded by symbols of patriotism, President Grover Cleveland spoke to a cheering crowd at the dedication of the Statue of Liberty in October, 1886.

HER CROWNING GLORY

Lady Liberty, as the statue is sometimes called, is more than just a **hollow** form—she has an **interior** that people can enter. Stairs lead to the top of the statue and to the twenty-five windows set in her crown. Many people think that the crown's seven points, or rays, represent the seven seas and seven continents of the world. However, they are actually meant to form a halo, as a reminder that the sculpture is divine, or holy.

The statue was a gift from France to the United States symbolizing the bond of friendship between the two nations. However, in time it would come to mean much more. The Statue of Liberty would become an enduring symbol of freedom and democracy to Americans and people around the world.

Praising the statue on behalf of the nation, President Grover Cleveland said, "We will not forget that Liberty has made here her home; nor shall her chosen altar be neglected." The statue's dedication was heralded by a twenty-one-gun salute, followed later that evening with a spectacular ball. Everything was perfect.

Twenty-two flights of stairs lead to the statue's crown. Some visitors prefer a shorter trip—192 steps or an elevator—to the pedestal observation deck, which also offers a good view of New York Harbor.

AN IDEA IS BORN

The road to creating the Statue of Liberty, however, was far from perfect. It all began at a dinner party in France in 1865. The party, hosted by French historian and politician Professor Édourd-René de Laboulaye, was attended by an assortment of French statesmen and intellectuals. Among the guests was Frédéric-Auguste Bartholdi, a thirty-one-year-old sculptor who was a highly respected member of the art world.

During a lively discussion at dinner Laboulaye remarked on the significant friendship between France and the United States. During the American Revolution,

French sculptor Frédéric-Auguste Bartholdi would spend many years working on the Statue of Liberty, which would later be considered one of his best works.

AN OUTSTANDING ARTIST

Frédéric-Auguste Bartholdi was born on August 2, 1834, in Alsace, France. Bartholdi's mother, Charlotte, recognized his creative genius early on and encouraged her son's interest in art. While at first Bartholdi studied painting, he later became more interested in sculpture. Besides the Statue of Liberty, Bartholdi's other sculptures in the United States include the Bartholdi Fountain in the Botanic Garden in Washington, D.C. (left), and the Lafayette statue in New York City. He died in Paris on October 4, 1904, of tuberculosis.

Many people in France sympathized with the American cause for independence from Great Britain, leading the country to take up arms on behalf of the American colonists.

France had proved itself a valuable ally by supporting the American colonists in their fight for independence from Great Britain. It sent both funds and supplies to the colonists, and at times, French soldiers had fought alongside them, as well. A number of the colonists' victories may not have been possible without the help of the French fleet and army; therefore, France was instrumental in enabling the colonists to establish a government based on freedom and liberty. Laboulaye, as well as many others, longed to see a similar form of democracy in France. In a democracy the people choose their leaders in elections. But Napoleon III, who was the emperor of France at the time, would never allow this.

Laboulaye felt a "genuine flow of sympathy" between France and the United States and described the countries as "two sisters." Aware that the hundredth anniversary of the colonists' independence was just eleven years away, Laboulaye hoped to give the United States a special hundredth birthday present on behalf of France.

THE FRIENDSHIP CONTINUED

Even after the American Revolution the bond between France and the United States remained strong. The French were greatly saddened by President Abraham Lincoln's **assassination** in 1865. They felt that an important defender of equality was gone forever, as they had respected the stand he took against slavery. To show their sympathy, the people of France gave Mrs. Lincoln a gold medal with an **inscription** in French:

> Dedicated by French democracy to Lincoln, twice-elected
>
> President of the United States—honest Lincoln who
>
> abolished slavery, reestablished the union, and saved
>
> the Republic, without veiling the Statue of Liberty.

He decided that the gift should be a monument honoring liberty. Laboulaye explained that this monument would have a **dual** purpose. It would reinforce France's bond with America. In addition, the gift would stress to Napoleon III's regime that the French people were dedicated to the concept of liberty and equality.

BARTHOLDI'S CREATION

Bartholdi wrote that the seed for the Statue of Liberty was sown at the party that night. It is generally thought that Laboulaye's opinion influenced Bartholdi, who began thinking along the same lines. Nevertheless, actual plans for the monument did not begin for years. In July 1870, France

Édourd-René de Laboulaye proposed the building of a memorial to honor the bond between France and the United States.

declared war on Germany and the Franco-Prussian War began. Bartholdi served in the French Army, and art took a backseat as the sculptor fought for his country. By 1871 the war had ended, and Napoleon III had fallen.

Bartholdi is shown here in his studio in Paris around 1892. He favored large-scale sculptures and worked from small models.

Laboulaye and Bartholdi hoped that the time might be right for democracy to take root in France. They thought that creating the statue now might encourage others to see the value of such a system. Bartholdi is quoted as saying: "I will try to

glorify the Republic and Liberty over there [in the United States] in the hope that someday I will find it again here."

At first no one was sure what form the statue would take, but one thing was certain: If Bartholdi designed it, the monument was bound to be big. Nearly all of Bartholdi's pieces were created on a grand scale. Many people believed that the sculptor had been greatly influenced by what he saw when he visited Egypt. Impressed by the size of such structures as the pyramids and the Sphinx, Bartholdi longed for a sense of massiveness in his own work. His first public monument—**commissioned** when he was just eighteen—was a 12-foot (3.7-m) high statue of one of Napoleon's generals. Workmen had barely been able to remove the larger-than-life sculpture from Bartholdi's studio. Yet the work received a good deal of praise and helped establish its creator's reputation as an artist.

FINDING THE RIGHT PLACE

Bartholdi was excited about doing a sculpture for the United States. To explore how the Americans would feel

This illustration (below) shows a bird's eye view of New York Harbor, from lower Manhattan. Bartholdi said that the idea for Lady Liberty became clear when he got his first view of the harbor.

* * * *

In the years following its dedication, the statue had an overwhelming impact on **immigrants** arriving in New York. In the words of one person, ". . . she represented the big, powerful country that was to be our future home."

about it, Bartholdi headed for the U.S. in the summer of 1871. He hoped to drum up enthusiasm for the project as well as find an appealing location to display the work. Bartholdi spent most of his days on the voyage making sketches of different views of Lady Liberty. The sculptor had also brought along a small model of the proposed monument to give Americans a better idea of how the finished product would look.

Bartholdi did not have to look very far to find the perfect spot for Lady Liberty. He spied the ideal place for her as soon as his ship entered New York Harbor. It was Bedloe's Island, one of a group of small islands in the harbor. At one time, the Mohegan Indians had called the island Minnissais, which

Bedloe's Island, an abandoned military post, was chosen as the future home for the Statue of Liberty.

means "Lesser Island," because it was so small. Despite its small size, the island seemed perfect for the project because New York Harbor was an active seaport where this tribute to liberty would get the attention it deserved. The French sculptor further described the location as a place "where people [immigrants] get their first view of the New World." He wanted them to see the statue before anything else.

SELLING THE IDEA

Finding a suitable site for the monument was just one phase of Bartholdi's mission. Creating a sense of enthusiasm for the statue among Americans proved to be much more difficult. Laboulaye had supplied the young sculptor with letters of introduction to a number of important Americans. Bartholdi met with President Ulysses S. Grant and

American literary figures, including Henry Wadsworth Longfellow, to talk about the project.

Although Bartholdi managed to pique the curiosity of some Americans, few appeared very enthusiastic. While the statue was to be a gift from the French, Americans would have to help finance it. Most of the people Bartholdi spoke to were not especially anxious to part with their money to make his dream come true. When Bartholdi returned to France, both he and Laboulaye agreed that they were not ready to begin construction.

This photograph features Bartholdi's first model of the statue's head, made of bronze.

The two Frenchmen made another attempt to get financial backing for the monument in 1874. They proposed dividing the cost of the monument between France and the United States. France would pay for the statue itself, while America was to pay for its pedestal and foundation. To speed things along, in 1875 Laboulaye formed the Franco-American Union, which included people from France as well as the United States. This organization worked to bring in **donations** on both sides of the Atlantic.

Though the original goal of completing the statue for the hundredth birthday (July 4, 1876) of the United States seemed unlikely, the group still did its best to meet that deadline. Appeals for donations for the statue appeared in the French press by the fall of 1875. The Franco-American Union proved quite creative in its fund-raising efforts. Banquets and balls were held in several French cities. The food and ballrooms for these occasions were donated, and all admission fees went to the statue's fund. Bartholdi came up with just enough money to begin work on Lady Liberty.

BUILDING LADY LIBERTY

Creating such a large sculpture was a tremendous undertaking. Bartholdi worked with a wide range of craftsmen. Metalsmiths were essential in creating the statue's framework and **exterior**. Carpenters, plasterers, painters, and others were needed to build the statue's "walk-in" interior.

It was crucial that the best material be selected for the statue's construction. Both stone and bronze seemed like good choices for Lady Liberty, but neither was right for the task. They were both too heavy to ship across the Atlantic.

In the end, copper was chosen. Copper is light, easy to work with, and strong enough to withstand the rough sea voyage to America. It was also thought that the material was less likely to be damaged by the salty-air environment of New York Harbor. At first, the statue would be a shiny orange-brown color, like a piece of new copper piping. In time, however, exposure to the elements would turn the copper an attractive blue-green color, which would blend in well with the harbor landscape.

A tremendous amount of work went into the statue's construction. Workmen hammered and pressed thin sheets of copper into shape using a series of increasingly larger molds, so that the statue grew larger as additional layers were added. More than three hundred individual copper sheets were needed to create Lady Liberty's outer form. Due to its immense size, the statue was made in hundreds of smaller segments and held together by rivets, or strong metal bolts.

Large numbers of French craftsmen were employed to build the Statue of Liberty. Only small portions of the statue could be worked on at a time.

Carpenters made wooden molds of each section, onto which copper sheets were pressed and hammered.

An engineer was hired to work with Bartholdi in designing a strong skeletal, or inner, framework to support the statue. This was vital because the statue was expected to last for centuries. The person selected for this job was a highly respected structural engineer named Gustave Eiffel. Known as the Magician of Iron, Eiffel had been extremely

18

innovative in using iron to build a number of large bridges. Now he turned his attention to devising a huge iron skeleton for Lady Liberty.

Gustave Eiffel was a talented engineer who, at the time, was primarily known for designing bridges.

QUITE A TOWER

In 1889, Gustave Eiffel would become famous for designing the Eiffel Tower (left) in Paris, France—one of the best known landmarks in the world. The Eiffel Tower has nearly six million visitors each year. Maintenance teams are always busy keeping the tower clean because it is so big. Each year, they use 4 tons of paper towels and 25,000 garbage bags, as well as many other cleaning supplies.

A portion of the statue's arm and the torch were displayed at the International Centennial Exhibition in Philadelphia. The exhibition, held in celebration of the country's hundredth birthday, was a tribute to the great strides made in science, industry, and international relations.

A MONUMENT TAKES SHAPE

Bartholdi was not able to complete the statue in time for America's centennial, or hundredth birthday. But the statue's raised arm and torch were finished by the summer of 1876. This portion of the statue was shipped to the United States to give Americans a taste of what was to come. The piece arrived just as the International Centennial Exhibition in Philadelphia, Pennsylvania, was taking place, so it was exhibited there. The statue's 30-foot (9.1-m) arm and torch were quite a hit, as most visitors had never seen a piece of sculpture that was large enough to hold a group of people inside.

Following the Philadelphia exposition, the arm and torch were displayed in New York City at Madison Square Park. For just fifty cents each, visitors could climb a ladder inside the statue's arm, which led to the balcony encircling her torch. People enjoyed exploring the oversized sculpture. For the first time, genuine enthusiasm for the statue began to take root in the United States.

Before long, additional parts of the statue were completed. Lady Liberty's shiny copper head was displayed at the Paris Universal Exposition of 1878. By

Bartholdi's mother, shown here, was the model for the statue's face.

then Bartholdi had begun calling the sculpture "My daughter, Liberty." However, Bartholdi's mother was actually the model for the statue's face.

Crowds in Paris loved the sculpture. Yet the problem that plagued the project from the start still existed—there never seemed to be enough money. That meant the Franco-American Union had to step up its fund-raising efforts. This time, several lotteries were held to bring in more cash. A lottery is a means of raising money by selling people tickets for the chance to win a prize. Items donated as lottery prizes included a beautiful set of silver plates, several pieces of jewelry, an oil painting, and two smaller sculptures by Bartholdi.

Modern-day miniatures of the statue are still popular collectibles.

When that failed to bring in enough cash, the Franco-American Union came up with yet another idea. It made small clay miniatures of the statue, which were sold as collectibles. Each model had the Franco-American Union's seal on it, and buyers could get their family's name engraved on the small replica, or copy. The miniatures sold for three thousand dollars (one thousand francs in France) each and were quite popular. At the close of 1879 it looked as if sufficient money might have been raised to finish the statue.

Bartholdi set to work in earnest on the project, and before long, substantial parts of the huge monument began to take shape. In a letter dated December 19, 1882, he wrote to the

chairman of the American Committee of the Franco-American Union to report on his progress. "Our work advances. The statue commences to reach above the houses, and by next spring we shall see it overlook the entire city, as the large monuments of Paris now do."

On behalf of the United States, Levi P. Morton accepted the statue as a gift in Paris.

★ ★ ★ ★

FINISHED—AT LAST!

The statue was finally completed by June of 1884. On the Fourth of July it was formally presented to Levi P. Morton, the minister of the United States to France. Accepting the

★ ★ ★ ★

gift in Paris on behalf of the American people, Morton said, "God grant that it [the statue] may stand until the end of time as an emblem of imperishable sympathy and affection

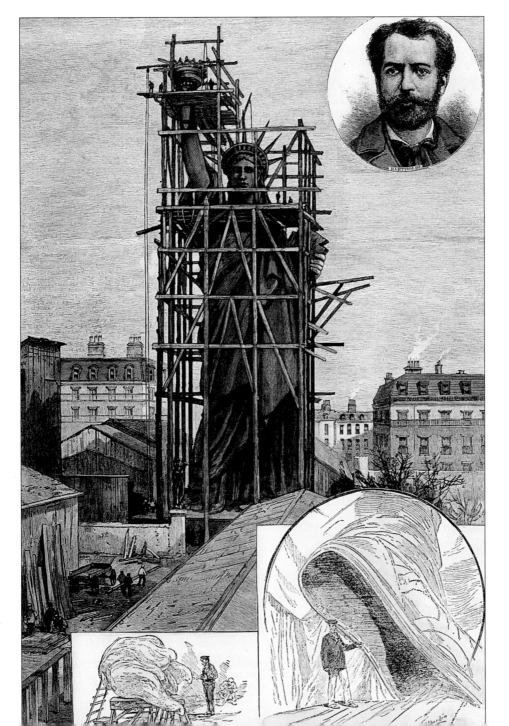

The statue was displayed in Paris before being shipped to the United States.

- Winds of 50 miles per hour (80 kilometers per hour) cause the body of the Statue of Liberty to sway up to 3 inches (7.6 centimeters) while the torch sometimes sways up to 5 inches (12.7 cm). This doesn't mean that the statue is unstable. Buildings and large monuments have traditionally been designed this way to withstand wind.

- It takes 354 steps to reach the crown, and 192 steps to reach the top of the pedestal.

- The twenty-five windows in the crown represent the number of gemstones, or "natural minerals," found on Earth. They also stand for heaven's rays of light shining over the world.

between the Republic of France and the United States." Lady Liberty was displayed in France before being sent to America, and the statue soon began to draw large crowds. Thousands of French citizens came to see it before it was shipped to its final destination in the United States.

Bartholdi and Laboulaye's dream was finally being realized. Sadly, Laboulaye died in 1883, before the statue's completion. But Bartholdi anxiously awaited the day when his masterpiece would be mounted on its pedestal. The French sculptor had no idea, however, that things were not so rosy across the Atlantic. In fact, while Bartholdi had been putting the final touches on his creation, a vital piece of the project—Lady Liberty's pedestal—remained unfinished.

THE MISSING PEDESTAL

The delay stemmed from the usual problem—lack of funding. Donations for the Statue of Liberty's pedestal had fallen far below expectations. Many Americans had mixed feelings about the structure, but most felt that its estimated cost was too high.

The statue's promoters tried without success to get the government to pay for it. Congress failed to approve a bill that would have provided one hundred thousand dollars for

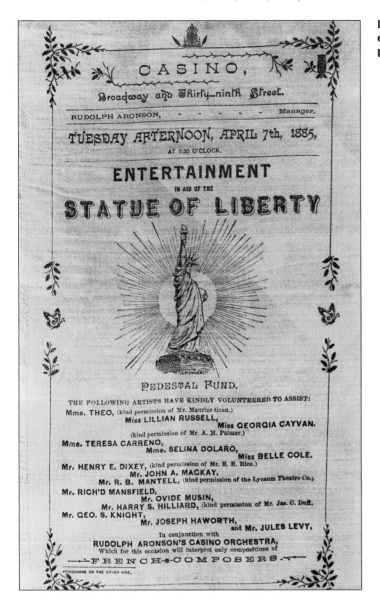

CASINO,
Broadway and Thirty-ninth Street.

RUDOLPH ARONSON, - - - - - Manager.

TUESDAY AFTERNOON, APRIL 7th, 1885,
AT 1:30 O'CLOCK.

ENTERTAINMENT
IN AID OF THE
STATUE OF LIBERTY

PEDESTAL FUND.

THE FOLLOWING ARTISTS HAVE KINDLY VOLUNTEERED TO ASSIST:
Mme. THEO, (kind permission of Mr. Maurice Grau.)
Miss LILLIAN RUSSELL,
Miss GEORGIA CAYVAN.
(kind permission of Mr. A. M. Palmer.)
Mme. TERESA CARRENO,
Mme. SELINA DOLARO,
Miss BELLE COLE.
Mr. HENRY E. DIXEY, (kind permission of Mr. E. E. Rice.)
Mr. JOHN A. MACKAY,
Mr. R. B. MANTELL, (kind permission of the Lyceum Theatre Co.)
Mr. RICH'D MANSFIELD,
Mr. OVIDE MUSIN,
Mr. HARRY S. HILLIARD, (kind permission of Mr. Jas. O. Duff.
Mr. GEO. S. KNIGHT,
Mr. JOSEPH HAWORTH,
and Mr. JULES LEVY,
In conjunction with
RUDOLPH ARONSON'S CASINO ORCHESTRA,
Which for this occasion will interpret only compositions of
— FRENCH * COMPOSERS —

PROGRAMME ON THE OTHER SIDE.

In the United States, theatrical events, art exhibitions, and auctions were some of the events planned to raise money for the statue's pedestal.

the pedestal. The state of New York tried to help out by allotting a fifty-thousand-dollar grant. (A grant is a sum of money that may be given by the government for a particular purpose.) However, the funds never came through because the governor vetoed, or rejected, it.

27

Although the Statue of Liberty was to remain permanently in the United States, it was difficult to convince most Americans to donate money to the project. People tended to think of Lady Liberty as a statue belonging to the state of New York rather than a national monument. They argued that New Yorkers should foot the bill. Meanwhile, the price was too steep for New York residents to meet without help.

In response, the American Committee of the Franco-American Union held a number of fund-raisers. They sponsored theatrical events, art shows, auctions, and even prize fights. Unfortunately, these efforts failed to bring in much money. By 1884 things had nearly hit rock bottom. Some wondered if Lady Liberty would ever reach New York Harbor.

Joseph Pulitzer, a talented Hungarian-American newspaper publisher, came to the U.S. in 1864. He would later be known for creating the Pulitzer Prize, an award for excellence in journalism, letters, and music.

PULITZER TO THE RESCUE

It was Joseph Pulitzer, owner of the *New York World* newspaper, who came to the statue's rescue. Pulitzer hoped that he could save the statue and boost his newspaper's circulation at the same time. He printed the following challenge in the *New York World* to urge his readers to act: "The *[New York] World* is the people's paper and now it appeals to the people to come forward and raise the money [for Lady Liberty's pedestal]." Noting that the statue had been paid for by "the masses of the French people," Pulitzer encouraged *New York World* readers to do the same with the statue's pedestal. "Let us respond in like manner. Let us not wait for the millionaires to give this money. It is not a gift from the millionaires of France to the millionaires of America, but a

✷ ✷ ✷ ✷

gift of the whole people of France to the whole people of America." Pulitzer also promised to publish the names of all who gave, no matter how small the donation.

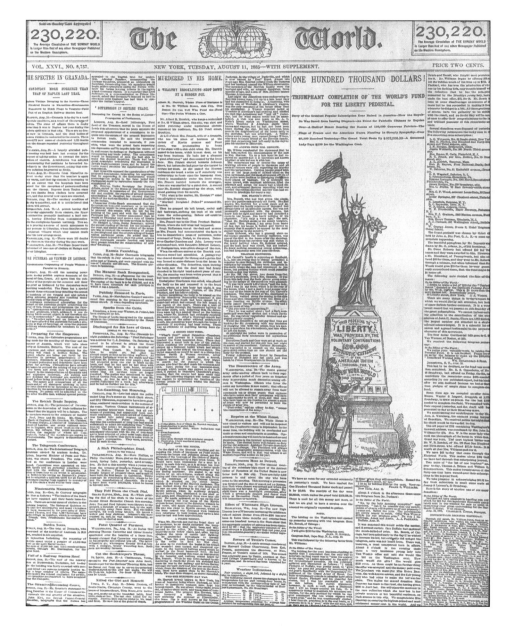

Richard Morris Hunt designed the pedestal. Hunt, who designed mansions for the wealthy, had a reputation for excellence.

The newspaper owner further argued that the Statue of Liberty was not a regional monument but instead stood for ideals common to all Americans. A number of African American newspapers followed the *New York World*'s lead in encouraging donations. These publications connected the statue's symbolic message of freedom and liberty with the end of slavery.

Americans heard the call and acted accordingly. The *New York World*'s circulation rose by almost fifty thousand readers. Many of these individuals were inspired by Pulitzer's plea. They began donating whatever they could for the cause. Elderly people sent in dollar bills, while children emptied their piggy banks. School classes collected money for the pedestal. By the summer of 1885 Pulitzer's $100,000 goal for the pedestal had been reached. The *New York World* reported that the money was the result of 121,000 individual contributions.

FINISHING UP

Once financial backing for the statue's pedestal was secured, the project's pace quickened. The architect selected to design the pedestal was a well-known American home designer named Richard Morris Hunt. The **granite** pedestal he created for the statue was built in the center of the eleven-pointed star-shaped walls that had once been part of Fort Wood. Fort Wood had been built on Bedloe's Island in the early 1800s to defend New York against naval attacks. Hunt's 89-foot (27.1-m) pedestal rested on a concrete foundation. To support the massive statue, the foundation

BARTHOLDI.

The pedestal was built in the center of Fort Wood.

contained 24,000 tons (24,385 metric tons) of concrete, setting a record for the largest amount of concrete ever poured for a single structure.

Meanwhile, in France the massive undertaking of **dismantling** and packing up the monument was well under way. The statue finally arrived at Bedloe's Island on June 17, 1885. It had been transported from France to the United

A MONUMENTAL TASK

The Statue of Liberty's pedestal is among the heaviest pieces of masonry ever constructed. When it was finally completed on April 22, 1886, the exuberant group of workers tossed their own coins into the **mortar** in celebration.

Crowds of cheering Americans watched as the *Isere* approached New York Harbor carrying the many pieces of the Statue of Liberty.

States on the French **frigate** *Isere*. The 350 individual pieces of the statue came carefully wrapped and labeled in 214 specially designed wooden crates. Some of the crates weighed just a few hundred pounds, while others weighed several tons. It took several months to uncrate and assemble the pieces of the statue, but it was worth the wait. The finished product was a tremendous source of pride for the country and made everyone's efforts seem worthwhile.

SHINING BRIGHT

The American public liked the idea of having the statue in the harbor, but before long, people noticed that the statue's torch did not shine as far out to sea as intended. That called for a change in Lady Liberty's lighting system. Through the years the statue's lighting would be enhanced a number of times as more technologically advanced equipment was developed. The torch's entire lighting system is equal to 2,500 times the effect of full moonlight.

The statue's lighting, which was a problem from the beginning, has been updated several times with more modern equipment.

In addition to having a formal dedication ceremony on October 28, 1886, more than twenty thousand people took part in a parade that day in honor of this special event. It's estimated that despite rainy weather, more than one million people came out to see the marchers. Everyone was excited about the statue.

FOR LIBERTY'S SAKE

ENLIST IN THE NAVY

A NATIONAL SYMBOL

Americans came to love the statue; it grew to be a national symbol of freedom, liberty, and justice. The statue even appeared on U.S. government posters and in advertising campaigns. Many people thought of her as the nation's female equivalent to Uncle Sam. (Uncle Sam is a fictional male character with a white goatee and a star-spangled suit often used to symbolize the United States government.) In 1924 President Calvin Coolidge declared the statue a national monument. By then, many Americans felt that the statue was a national treasure.

In 1903 a small but important addition was made to the Statue of Liberty. This addition was a bronze plaque with a poem inscribed on it. The poem,

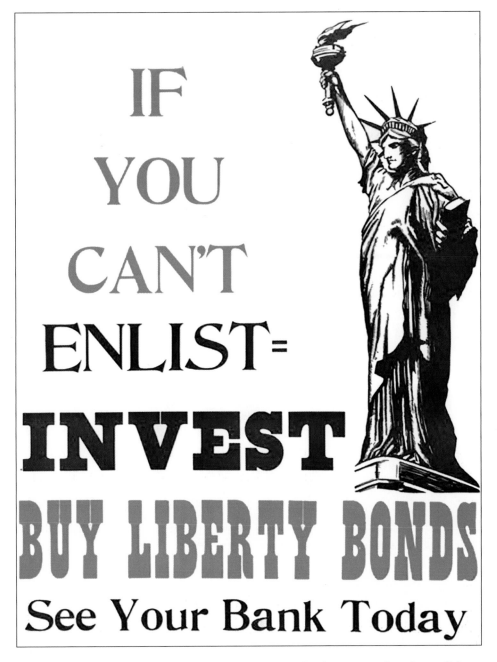

Because the statue inspires feelings of pride and passion in so many Americans, it has been used successfully in advertising campaigns throughout the years. The posters shown here and at left were created during World War I to encourage Americans to enlist in the Navy and to buy Liberty Bonds.

THE NEW COLOSSUS.

NOT LIKE THE BRAZEN GIANT OF GREEK FAME,
WITH CONQUERING LIMBS ASTRIDE FROM LAND TO LAND;
HERE AT OUR SEA-WASHED, SUNSET GATES SHALL STAND
A MIGHTY WOMAN WITH A TORCH, WHOSE FLAME
IS THE IMPRISONED LIGHTNING, AND HER NAME
MOTHER OF EXILES. FROM HER BEACON-HAND
GLOWS WORLD-WIDE WELCOME; HER MILD EYES COMMAND
THE AIR-BRIDGED HARBOR THAT TWIN CITIES FRAME.
"KEEP ANCIENT LANDS, YOUR STORIED POMP!"
    CRIES SHE
WITH SILENT LIPS. "GIVE ME YOUR TIRED, YOUR
    POOR,
YOUR HUDDLED MASSES YEARNING TO BREATHE FREE,
THE WRETCHED REFUSE OF YOUR TEEMING SHORE.
SEND THESE, THE HOMELESS, TEMPEST-TOST TO ME,
I LIFT MY LAMP BESIDE THE GOLDEN DOOR!"

———

THIS TABLET, WITH HER SONNET TO THE BARTHOLDI STATUE
OF LIBERTY ENGRAVED UPON IT, IS PLACED UPON THESE WALLS
IN LOVING MEMORY OF
EMMA LAZARUS
BORN IN NEW YORK CITY, JULY 22D. 1849
DIED NOVEMBER 19TH. 1887.

The poem written on this bronze plaque welcomes immigrants to America.

called "The New Colossus" or "Mother of Exiles," was written by Emma Lazarus, an established poet who was moved by the plight of immigrants. The poem serves as a welcoming message from the Statue of Liberty to people coming to the United States from throughout the world. At the time it was written, most immigrants arrived in the United States through New York Harbor. Therefore, the Statue of Liberty was one of the first things they saw. It reads:

Not like the brazen giant of Greek fame,
With conquering limbs astride from land to land;
Here at our sea-washed, sunset gates shall stand
A mighty woman with a torch, whose flame
Is the imprisoned lightning, and her name
Mother of Exiles. From her beacon-hand
Glows world-wide welcome; her mild
*   eyes command*
The air-bridge harbor that twin
*   cities frame.*
"Keep ancient lands, your
*   storied pomp!" cries she*
With silent lips. "Give me
*   your tired, your poor,*
Your huddled masses
*   yearning to breathe free,*
The wretched refuse of
*   your teeming shore,*
Send these, the homeless,
*   tempest-tost to me,*
I lift my lamp beside the
*   golden door!"*

Emma Lazarus originally wrote "The New Colossus" in 1883 for an auction to raise money for the statue's pedestal.

The immigrants who came to America were again remembered in 1936, when a fiftieth anniversary celebration of the unveiling of the Statue of Liberty was held. At the ceremony President Franklin D. Roosevelt said:

> Millions of men and women . . . adopted this homeland because in this land they found a home in which the things they desired most could be theirs—freedom of opportunity, freedom of thought, freedom to worship God. Here they found life because here there was freedom to live. It is the memory of all these eager, seeking millions that makes this one of America's places of great romance. . . . It is fitting therefore that this should be a service of rededication to the liberty and the peace which this statue symbolizes. Liberty and peace are living things. In each generation—if they are to be maintained—they must be guarded and vitalized anew.

In keeping with that sentiment, steps have been taken to properly maintain the statue. By the 1980s

Once the gateway for more than twelve million immigrants entering the United States, Ellis Island now serves as a museum, telling the story of all those who passed through its doors.

ELLIS ISLAND

Ellis Island lies north of the Statue of Liberty. More than 12 million immigrants passed through the immigration center there when they came to America in search of a better life. Due to its historical importance, Ellis Island was declared part of the Statue of Liberty National Monument in 1965.

In the 1980s, the statue underwent a facelift in preparation for her centennial birthday celebration in July 1986.

time and weather had taken its toll on the monument, and some repairs needed to be done. Money was collected through donations for a multimillion-dollar **restoration** project that took about two years to complete.

All the repairs were completed for the statue's hundredth birthday. On July 4, 1986, the Statue of Liberty was the centerpiece of a fabulous festival that lasted four days. Standing at the monument, President Ronald Reagan stated: "We are the keepers of the flame of liberty; we hold it high for the world to see." That night there was a light show over the harbor and a magnificent fireworks display lit up the sky. Television viewers around the world saw the statue in its full glory.

A second ceremony was held at the Statue of Liberty on October 28, 1986, to mark the one-hundred-year anniversary of the statue's original dedication. When the statue had first gone up in the United States, Bartholdi looked at the finished product with pleasure. He is quoted as saying, "The dream of my life is accomplished." If he were alive today, he'd be pleased to see how much his dream has come to mean to all Americans.

Fireworks burst around the Statue of Liberty during the spectacular celebration of a national monument.

Glossary

assassination—the murder of a well-known or
    important person

commissioned—having been assigned to do something

dedication—the unveiling or opening of a new structure
    or building with a ceremony

dismantling—taking something apart

donation—money or goods given to a charity or
    other cause

dual—having two sides or uses

exterior—the outside of a structure

frigate—a type of sea vessel used until the early
    twentieth century

granite—a hard gray rock used as a building material

hollow—something with an empty space inside it

immigrant—a person who leaves his or her home country to settle in a different country

innovative—a new idea or approach

inscription—a carved, written, or engraved saying or message

interior—the inside of a structure

monument—a statue or other structure built to honor someone or something

mortar—a cement mixture used for building

restoration—the process of making something look as it did originally by repairing or retouching it

symbolic—something that stands for something else

tyranny—the unjust and cruel exercise of power

Timeline: The Statue of

1865	1870	1871	1875	1876	1877	1878
 Professor Édourd-René de Laboulaye suggests the idea for a statue honoring liberty.	France declares war on Germany, and the Franco-Prussian War begins. Sculptor Frédéric-Auguste Bartholdi serves in the military.	Bartholdi goes to America to look for a site for the Statue of Liberty and win America's support for the project.	The Franco-American Union is formed.	The Statue of Liberty's arm and torch are displayed in Philadelphia and New York City.	 Congress approves Bedloe's Island as the site for the statue.	The Statue of Liberty's head is displayed at the Paris Universal Exposition of 1878.

Liberty

1880	**1883**	**1884**	**1885**	**1886**	**1903**	**1924**

Gustave Eiffel designs the framework for the Statue of Liberty.

Laboulaye dies before the statue's completion.

The finished statue is presented to the American people at a ceremony in Paris. It is displayed in France before being shipped to the United States.

The statue is dismantled and shipped to America.

The Statue of Liberty is assembled in the United States and dedicated in October.

The poem "The New Colossus" is inscribed on a plaque for the Statue of Liberty.

The Statue of Liberty is made a national monument.

1956	**1965**	**1984**	**1986**

The name of Bedloe's Island is changed to Liberty Island.

Ellis Island is made part of the Statue of Liberty National Monument.

Broad-scale repairs begin on the statue.

Lady Liberty is one hundred years old. The statue's centennial is celebrated on the Fourth of July.

On October 28, the one hundredth anniversary of the statue's original dedication is celebrated.

To Find Out More

BOOKS AND VIDEOS

Bierman, Carol. *Journey to Ellis Island*. New York: Hyperion Press, 1998.

Curlee, Lynn. *Liberty*. New York: Atheneum, 2000.

Freedman, Russell. *Immigrant Kids*. Glenview, Ill.: Scott Foresman, 1995.

Maestro, Betsy C. *Coming to America: The Story of Immigration*. New York: Scholastic, 1999.

ONLINE SITES

Ellis Island
http://www.internationalchannel.com/education/ellis/

Statue of Liberty, National Park Service
http://www.nps.gov/stli/

Learning Adventures in Citizenship, The Statue of Liberty
http://www.pbs.org/wnet/newyork/laic/

Index

Bold numbers indicate illustrations.

About the Author

Award-winning author **Elaine Landau** received a bachelor's degree in English and journalism from New York University and a master's degree in library and information science from Pratt Institute. She worked as a newspaper reporter, children's book editor, and a youth services librarian before becoming a full-time writer. She has written more than two hundred nonfiction books for children and young adults. She lives in Miami, Florida, with her husband, Norman, and their son, Michael.